birds & other dreamers

poems

k.b. marie

This book is a product of the author's imagination. Any references to historical events, real people, or real places have been used fictitiously. Other names, characters, places, and incidents are also the product of the author's imagination. Any resemblance to actual persons, living or dead, business establishments, events, or locales is entirely coincidental.

No part of this book shall be reproduced or transmitted in any form or by any means without prior written permission of the publisher. Although every precaution has been taken in preparation of the book, the publisher and the author assume no responsibility for errors or omissions. Neither is any liability assumed for damages resulting from the use of information contained in this book or its misuse.

Copyright © 2020 K.B. Marie
Illustrations by Victoria Solomon
Formatting by Jasie Gale
All rights reserved.

Grateful acknowledgment is made to the *Oklahoma Review*, in whose pages the poem "Timberlane Street" first appeared.

ISBN-13: 978-1-949577-29-7
ISBN-10: 1-949577-29-5

birds & other dreamers

table of contents

dedication

preface: a comet, dreaming   9

I.
two kinds of dreams   15
preparations   16
today, when the postman came   17
I sing you to me   19
timberlane street   20
devotion and other types of melancholy   22
houses   24
begin   25
in the making   27
sunflowers   29
your first   30
love as source of heat   31
yet you drive me crazy   32
you never asked to be a page boy   34
boundaries   35
two kayaks   36
everything but you   38
cloud gate   39

II.
the beach   45
this smile, before   46
someone cries in my dreams   48
getting lost in distraction city   50
beneath it all   51
purpose   52
then & now   53

dark water	54
when the fear comes	56
choices	59
begonia	60
opaque	61
first snow	62
you love me better	64
an egg	66

III.
the inevitable	71
while you work in the garden	73
the end of summer	74
in the name of love	75
first light	77
thinking ahead	78
iloilo city	81
the waking	83
first date	84
grief	86
the leap	88
white crane	90
the wind	91
how I knew	93
evening star	95
love through the ages	97

author's note
also by k.b. marie
about the author
about the illustrator

For Kimberly Benedicto,
always

preface: a comet, dreaming

This is the dream.

I am a comet,
stardust breath
and spectral tail ablaze.
In the blackest corner of
a starless sky,
I pace alone.
Through a forgotten orbit
out of desperation
for the familiar,
in loyalty to a rhythm
I cannot comprehend,
a millennium at a time.

Infinity.

You are born, and in that
instant my comet heart hears
the first notes of our song
and sets course for Earth.

By the power of dream
logic somehow
ice is exchanged for bone.

Stardust settles into green eyes.

Still it takes me 27 years
to move this body
into your orbit. But the
homecoming feels familiar,
expected, as if I've only
just left and come back having
forgotten something

important, until I wake
crying, begging. *I don't want to
return to the cold dark
of space alone.* Explaining
I can't bear to spend another
millennium out there, knowing
you may or may not be born,

knowing orbits can change
and I will have to lose you again—
search for you again.

In our bed, you smile. You
kiss each wet cheek and tell me
it was only a dream.

But it isn't, I say.
This life is the dream.

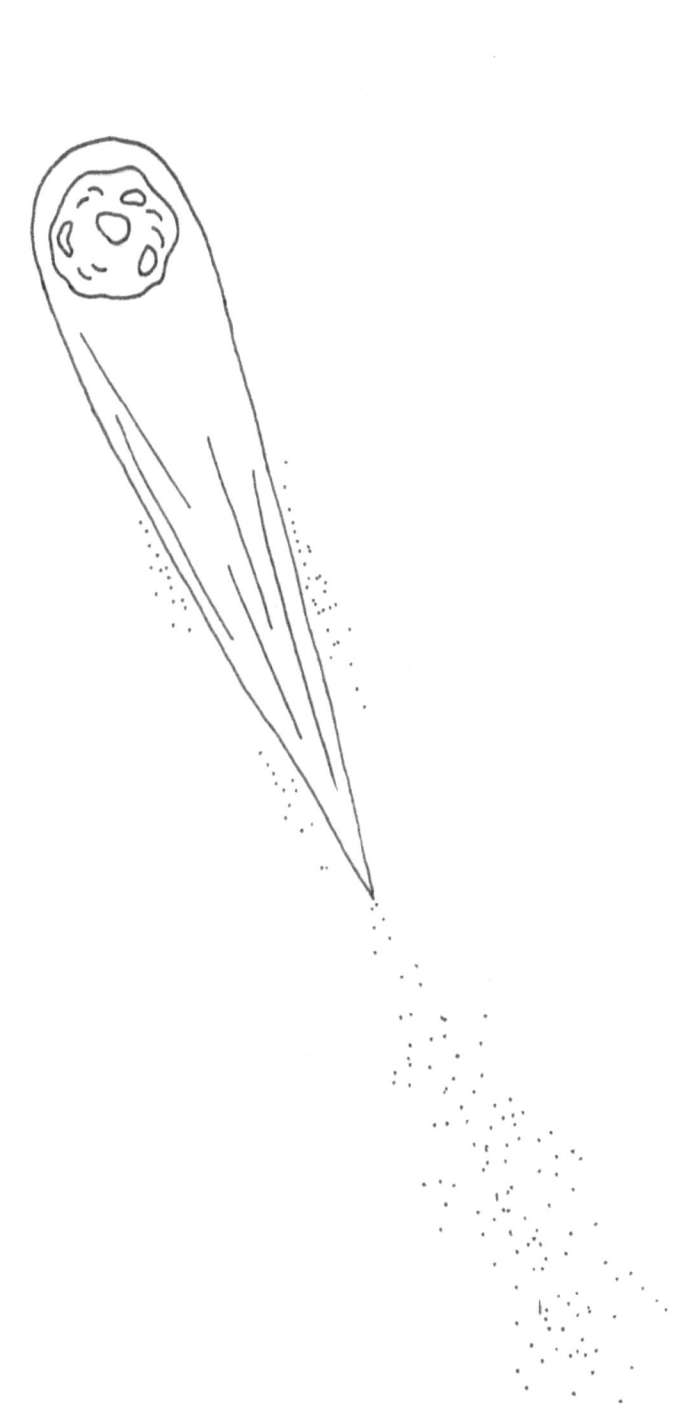

I.

two kinds of dream

A bug flies into a clear pane of glass.
He bounces back, stunned.
Loving you was like that.

You were simply there. And before—
I don't remember *before*
except as a dream, troublesome,

from which I woke feeling sick
with fear and longing, those twin fists
clenching deep inside me.

For now, it is all incandescent sunlight
and the sounds of birds building
nests in the gutters. Robins sing

in the misty morning, and a frog leaps
into the high grass as you kiss me
before my eyes even open.

If this is a dream, let me never wake.
If this is a dream, I must dream deeper.

preparations

I begin with the bird feeder. I try
to shake all the dropped seeds
from its crevices and refill it.

I wash out the bird bath, use
my hand to wipe the glass clean
before adding crystalline water.

I do all of this so the birds will come
and I can sit by the window
and watch them sing, dance, and
conspire with each other.

Sometimes
a rabbit comes. Often squirrels,
or chipmunks.

It's amazing, isn't it?

How often, when aiming our love,
the universe gives us more
than what we ask for.

today, when the postman came

He delivered a book I'd been expecting,
and a bill I had not.

We put things into the box. Things come back.

What we send out into the universe,
what comes back, and what doesn't…

It's the forces unseen who decide this, isn't it?
Or how much of our own agency

plays its part? I wonder
about us. Every time I place a kiss behind

your ear, or a hand on your knee,
or if I walk through

the house calling your name,
if I put down this poem when you call mine—

What are we sending out into the universe
each time we love each other?

What, I wonder, is on its way to us even now?

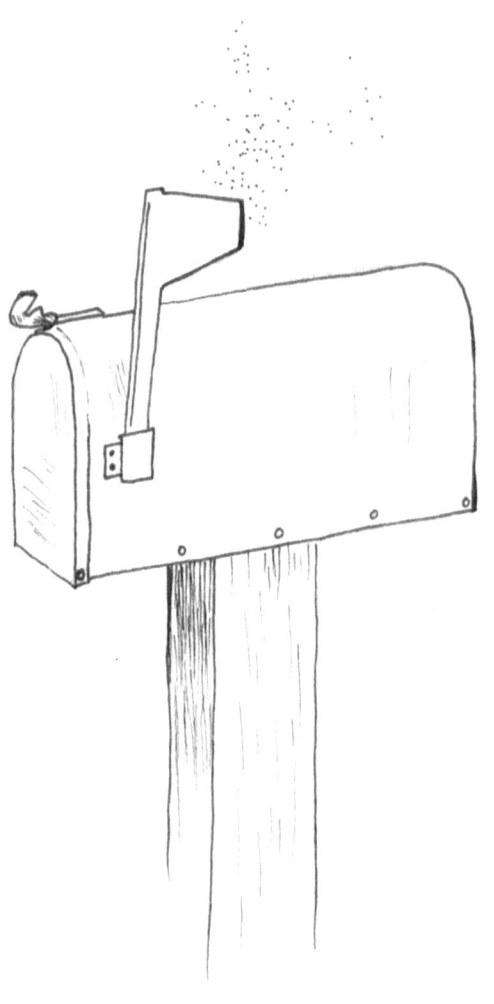

I sing you to me

Cardinals perch on the feeders, spitting
black seeds from their beaks.

Chipmunks run in and out
of the rainspouts. Spiders nest

in the corners of our rooms and
for some reason, the mailbox.

Crickets spring from the long grasses
as we pass. Bees sleep drunkenly

in the sunflowers you planted. And yes,
I carry the frogs away from your peonies.

When the hummingbird came
to the window last night, and you sat up

smiling to see it, I wondered—*Why us?*
There is so much love.

Is it these acts of sharing that bring life closer?
An unheard melody that sings *you're safe here?*

Or is it warmth, like an August sun?
A blanket laid on the grass. An invitation.

timberlane street

An upturned watch on the end table.
An empty water glass forgotten on the white
kitchen counter. Shoes side by side
nearest the door, laces entwined. Jackets
piled sleeve to sleeve, fabrics for every
possible weatherscape, all arranged just so.

Two desks lean cattycorner from one another,
each standing guard against a wall, and willing
to offer differing perspectives, their different
views of the white railings beyond the window,
the ones holding blood bursts of flowers
in wire coco-liner baskets, green vines reaching
as an inscribed sun-catcher splinters the light.

And like the oak, poplar, linden trees
surrounding our shared loft, their seasonal shift
from gold to white to green again, inside we
grow as well. Cupboards flower.

Closets fill, empty, and are filled again.
A bed warms each night and cools each day.

Mums give way to petunias, to tomatoes
and basil and the pictures lining the shelves
remind us of where we've been. And of those
whom we've brought with us—or haven't.

Borrowed books come and go and the most
loved are filed away between aging covers,
rounding out the bulging gut of an overstuffed
bookcase. And a small dog guards all, standing
on a bench, vigilant at the open window
for a trash truck or unsuspecting postal man,
while I stand at the kitchen sink, washing
out your forgotten water glass, contemplating
the press of your lips to its translucent rim
and the way sunlight brightens your eyes,

drawing out the fire until the rich amber
is a pale, glowing sepia. And the water droplets
echo in the metal basin like the ticking of a clock,
the minutes between *now* and *dinnertime*, my
impatience for the sound of your key in the door.

devotion and other types of melancholy

A little dog waits by the door.
It doesn't matter if you've been gone
for one hour or eight.

He will be there when you arrive
to jump and yip and turn circles
around your heels. His tail will wag
with the same fervor, no matter
how stiff his joints may be from
the waiting, no matter
how the separation may have
emptied his heart.

While he waits, I pick up socks.
And wash socks. And fold socks.
And put the socks in your drawer.

I make lists. Grocery lists. Number
lists of who we must call about
that leak in the basement.
Birthday lists and wish lists. And
lists of all the places I want to go
with you.

I work in the yard. There are the weeds
in your garden and the overgrown tree.
There's the grass, too, of course. And

the weedeater that has to be repaired
as soon as I find the pliers you've lost.

He waits.
I pick up socks. Work in the yard.

I love you, too, you know.

houses

You seed this house like you seed my heart. I find
traces of you everywhere. Discarded shoes,
a littering of chocolate foils. A scarf, still warm,
thrown over the back of a chair. I move
from room to room, collecting this evidence of you.

And yet I could not point to the muscle, to a vein
or ventricle and say—*here. This is where you are.*
These are the parts of me you have touched—
because still I discover you again and again.

Like a song, forgotten
until the melody is suddenly renewed
and all the lyrics are coming back to me now.

A tune fluttering on the wind has a way of blooming.

I breathe it in. I sing the chorus, listening
to its echo fill these halls, our bedroom, and even
rooms that had long ago been shut.

begin

I hear you calling
in the streets of Chicago.
The taxis honk and subways
screech. A jazz festival rabbits,
fever-pitched, down
a melody's path.
Bicycles trill.
The brakes of a bus sigh.
Children run, shoes slapping
pavement. Exasperated
mothers cry after them.
People laugh. Someone
shouts and the band
strikes up again.
All of this is not unlike
the cacophony of my mind,
a life, living lulls me
away from such moments
into the inner circus,
choreographed,
a song and dance.

And yet—your voice rises
above all, a singular cherubic
bell. Is it your call
that holds this magic?

Or have you always known
the best way to cut through?

in the making

Everything requires conditions:
the temperature of the water,
flavor of the blossoms.

Green. Ginger. Peach.

Then comes the patience,
a slow development.

Saturation denotes its strength.
Tea and love are the same
in this way and others.

A forgotten cup turns cold.
Too much delicacy is bitter on
the tongue. Both

when taken inside create
a warmth against the rain falling.

Which is to say, I know this
isn't a one-shot deal.
There is no *set it and forget it!*

You will be the first task
each morning. And the last
pleasure each night.

Time and tastes will change.
The ritual will not. What else

can I offer but a life of quiet
devotion? What else can

I promise except to savor you
until the last drop?

sunflowers

I want to remember you like this
as the girl who loved sunflowers.
The bright smile you wore
as you came into my office with a
fistful of sunny faces. Triumphant
in the knowledge you grew them
with your own two hands.

Aren't they beautiful?

In truth, I can't tell one glorious face
from another. Shine is shine.

Yes, I say, my eyes on you. *Very beautiful.*

your first

The redbuds are dancing.
Heart-shaped leaves lift and fall.
A harbinger, reminding us
to trust the power of one's own magic.

This is why I love seeing this *you*.
The writer. The lamenter.

Budding craftswoman.

When you bring me pages and say,
"Could you…?"
How can I resist? Later they might say

I did this. The gravity
of my own lexiconic orbit pulled
the words from you. We know better.
The truth:

The song was in you always.
And I was only the lucky soul
who heard those first, uncertain notes.

love as a source of heat

Geese call out coordinates
overhead. The squirrels build
into the walls. And birds fatten

themselves in the tall grasses
before nesting in our eaves.
It's that time again. To move

closer. It's been a long summer,
a verdant growing season.

And now I'm tired. Now I only

want to sleep beside you
and dream of first light.
But first there's this business

of bedding down, of settling in
by the fire. I think it's no surprise
I fell in love in autumn.

How could I have resisted?

With all that starburst gold,
and scarlet blazing around you?

yet you drive me crazy

When you place your shoes
in front of doorways.

When you leave a cabinet open
or a drawer ajar.

The clothes. *All* the clothes.
On floors and doors.

When you ask me to turn
down the air, then leave
the front door open.

When I clean the kitchen,
take a shower,
and return to discover
you've "made lunch."

When you complain that you
can't sleep, but also
turn to your phone at 3 a.m.

When you can't find *anything*
but also never put *anything* back.

When you begin a chore,
yet, somehow, get me to finish it.

When you wait until I'm
nearly dead before asking,
"Can't you do it?"

When you hide (hoard) things
in the secret places you don't
think I know about.

You've never made the bed,
or mowed the lawn,
or carried your own toads
from the garden.

When you say "*babe.*"
When you say, "I'll do it later."
When we both know you've
just lied.

But remember:
The robin, who has plucked
the worm from the soil,
has learned to love the taste
of dirt in her mouth.

She can't live any other way.
If there was no rain, no worms.

If there are no worms, she can
expect a slow and awful death.

you never asked to be a page boy

Can you bring me a cup of tea?
Also, a saucer for the bag.
And while you're up,
please check the laundry, let in
the dog, tell me what you want
to do about dinner.

Here we make a joke: *this is why you're
married when all your friends are single.*

But the truth is, I married you
because I love the way your lips
rest, soft and open, while you read.

I married you for your smile
and delight in all the surprising
ways I can summon and conjure it.

I married you because of how
your hand feels when it slips
into mine, or your arms hook
around my waist. I wanted to own
that smile, those hands.

So please forgive all my requests.
I only wanted to know that when
I call your name, you'll answer me.

boundaries

The honeysuckle is growing through
the fence. Stiff branches shove
into weakening planks.

And I, its mistress, should cut it back.

I can't bring myself to do it.
These days I'm remembering things
I understood as a child:

All that lives wants only to live free.

two kayaks

We put our boats into the river.
I have a concerned dog on my feet.
You have potato chips.

To each their own pleasures, and
my pleasure is found here,
set low in the water, a paddle

dipping side to side. It's true I
often pull out ahead of you.
It's true I'm propelled forward by

a current not entirely of my own
making. Even sand, if lifted,
dreams of long-ago shores.

I need to see the S-necked
heron on the riverbank.
The tortoise

slipping from the sunny rock
into the dark below. The cuckoo
calling out as its wings

skim the shimmering surface. I
cannot rest until I see everything.
I cannot rest until I am seen.

But I could never be so brave, so
headlong for this life, if
you were not so close behind me.

everything but you

I carry my fears in a heart-shaped pocket.
I war against them. I wield affirmations –

you're doing great! Keep going!

I cloak myself in dreams of steel spires.

I call forward the enchantments of
an organizational planner. Color-coded.

In all my preparations against the hardships
of uncertainty, your name does not appear.

This may seem callous, my love. Uncaring,
as if I have no place for you in this.

But why should I fear the sun falling
from the sky? What fool could imagine

the north star going dark forever?

cloud gate

In the hot Chicago sun, the bean shone
like a spaceship, temporarily parked
for human inspection. We circled it,
fingers trailing the iridescent surface,
our faces warped and replayed for us.

It begs the question, doesn't it?

What could possibly survive? Never
mind if it's antibiotic-resistant
disease, nuclear war, economic collapse
or the fascists that have moved in next
door. Think only of this place now.

Imagine wide boulevards, empty.
There will be no people to tend the tall,
overgrown buildings. Birds, if there are
still birds, will darken the sky.
They will be the ones who remember
our songs, our stories. The roots
will reclaim all: storefront windows,
split concrete, rusted rails, machines
no one can operate. And what of us?
When the world has ended,
when the world has moved on,
what will be left of us?

Of love?

Have I given you anything so substantial
as the John Hancock building?
A bronze statue in your honor? A street
in your name? Or a park where you can sit
and eat your ham and cheese crepes,
drink your iced coffee, and allow
the sunlight to dance in your hair?

Is anything we make, or offer, able
to survive this world or any other?
What does one do if the dream stops—

II.

the beach

At the water's edge, the surf roars.

It calls out favor, or warning,
depending. When I am here with you,
its melancholy. I hold within me

both truths: The sun shines. We're happy.
Clouds will come. Winter is spent alone.
I sit in that space,

in the Venn diagram of duality.
You are both here and not.

We are blessed. We are doomed
to part. You ask me: *Why do you
look so sad all of a sudden?* I force a smile,

while it is still mine. I take your hand
and pull you into the last of the waves.

this smile, before

Summers are timeless. It's the heat.
It presses on the mind like a gloved
hand. And tired minds consider stranger
things. I wonder if we've done this
before, in another life. You lay
on the chaise, sprawled as you are.
Perhaps there was also a pug.
And where was I?
In a suit? Or a dress? Did I ask
would you like some tea? Did I read
to you some amusing passage
from a book open? Did I reach
for the laugh as I do even now?
So much of this life echoes. Only…
I am not sure if we are names called
softly down the hall, or dark stones
thrown, and sinking
into the lake of all that's forgotten.

someone cries in my dreams

At the border, they take the children.
In the schools, they shoot the children.
Meanwhile I am here with you,

in a paradise, in a long, endless summer
of dappled sunlight. Delicate linden
blossoms fill the breeze.

What right do I have to kiss you
each morning? What right do I have
to lay down beside you each night?

You're at the table.
You're on the sofa beside me.
The point is, baby, I know

where you are. In my dreams
the ground opens up in our garden.
All that we've planted is swallowed

by what's been burrowing unseen
beneath. I am not surprised. Even
the children know comfort has its tithe.

But who is picking up this check
at the high-end sushi restaurant
we love? At Whole Foods

or Eddie Bauer, or the doctor's office,
at the airport—two tickets for London—
Japan? Who really pays for the books

filling three bedrooms, for the running
water in one and a half baths?
These can't be gifts. Free. Not for me.

But I try to believe it. And maybe
that's the sin. The damnation.
You turn toward me laughing.

The sun is in your hair—
It seems a shame that I can't see past
the shadows eclipsing your face.

getting lost in distraction city

You have your escape hatch and I have mine.
     Or really it's a collection of doors, isn't it? – and like the soul,
  it begins with the eyes. iPhone, iPad, I feel like
        there is a great distance building between us.
Your hand is on my thigh,
     or sometimes
  the bottom of your foot is pressed to the bottom of my foot,
  on the enormous sofa we had to disassemble
just to get in here.
  But as with all lovers, physical proximity is only part
     of the equation.
          Where are you, my love?
What has caused that smile
     to pass across your lips just now?
       When you meet my gaze, finally, of your own volition,
  it is with the same look I receive if I call your name.
 I *am* calling you.
     And I'm glad you're still listening. For now.
  So while you're near,
     tell me—
       Will there be a day when you can no longer hear me?

beneath it all

The dharma warns against fixed identities.
What does that mean for the *me*
sitting here, loving the *you*?

It's supposed to be reassuring, freer, that
we all have erroneous ideas. I think I know
who—what—you are. And don't.
You think you know who—what—I am.

But if *we* are made of plaster masks,
if *we* dance so well within the predrawn lines,
it begs the question, doesn't it?

Who am I loving?
Whose neck do I kiss at the kitchen sink?
Whose hip do I enjoy
squeezing, before pulling it into mine?

Where are you under all of that? And why
do I mourn the loss of us already? Why
bother, when I don't know what I have?

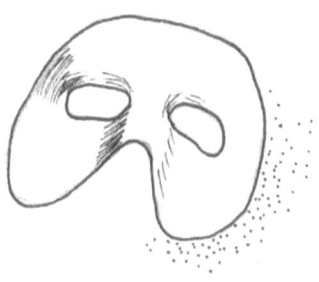

purpose

I work hard because I am afraid
and should you leave me, I want

to have something you-shaped, built
and ready to place on the sofa

beside me. Or do I work because
I am not worried—about you anyway.

The fears leading me down dark
corridors, away from the sound of

your voice sound like pages torn
from a favorite book.

Or do I work as a bee works?
Compulsively sifting

grains between soft hands, knowing
I have only one season to do it all.

A queen may rule, but it changes
nothing. The flowers can't sing

forever. The sunlight
can only hold out for so long.

then & now

I spend a lot of time alone. I choose this
now. As a neglected child, it was a given.

Writing requires an abandonment of
one's body and a traveling inward,

to the worlds where a body cannot go.
This is no loss to me.

But if one travels too far, one can forget
everything they have waiting for them—

Because magic cannot be contained, even
in a gentle hand. It becomes lonely work.

*

You push the knife through an apple.
You open and close the squeaky fridge door.

The dog beside me snores, turns over.
There's so much to be here for now.

Keep at it, my love. *Please.*
Keep reminding me it's safe to stay.

dark water

It would be so easy to sink. It takes
almost no weight these days
as the outside presses hard against us.

It isn't the cold,
which has a way of seizing the body.
Maybe it would be easier with cold.

Maybe then, I would have the sense
to pull back and protect myself.
But because it's warm I walk forward

into the knifepoint. Or more gently,
into a hand cupping my heart.
Sometimes the thought of you is enough.

Other times, it is as if I can't breathe or
the water will come rushing in.
They say it's all in the mind, this darkness.

But you're in here too.
I dream you are leaving. I dream of
coming home to an empty house.

I dream of being chased away from you.
Of you dead or dying, you screaming
my name.

I must believe
the hand I am holding won't turn to teeth.
It would help—if only I could see it.

when the fear comes

Sometimes the swarm finds me like this.
It moves in, buzzing. Becomes black rain

clouds thick and close enough to touch.
I cower in the center, consumed by

and afraid of—so many things.
But mostly I am afraid of how I can't

see a way out of this sudden endless night.

*

Then you call my name.

Clouds lift. Sunlight glints off the wet grass.
A morning. A blue-only sky. Oh,

if that were enough…
But I smell the rain. I feel the electric spark

of lightning along my skin.
I know a dark horizon when I see one.

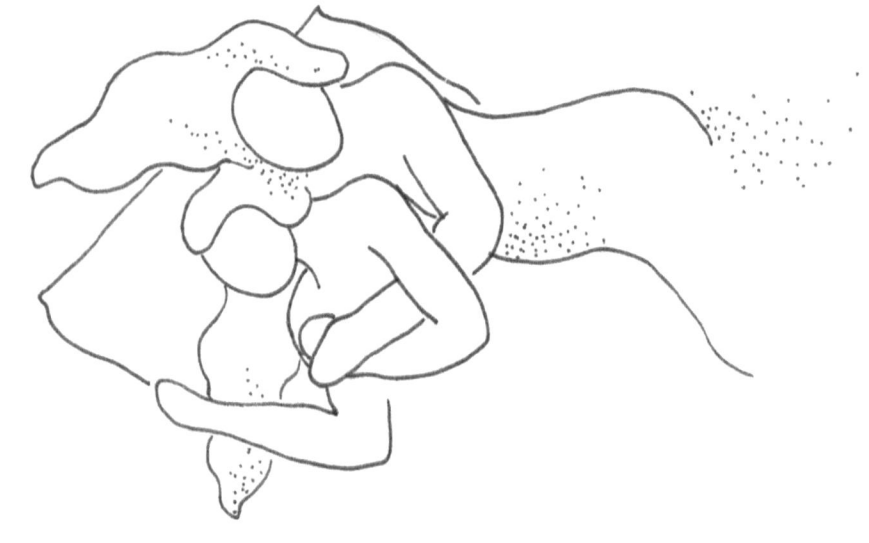

choices

The novels I read aren't romantic and so
the people are busy—with war, with revenge,
with the tedious nature
of their own transformations. All the while
I'm thinking *get back to her. We both know
your love story is the real story. Be together while you can.*

Yet the war carries on, the revenge is complete,
and our heroine finds one more journey to take:

I have books to write and a career to
fuss over. So I came to bed late again.
Bone tired. I put what was left of me on the bed
beside you. But my mind would not come back.
It was still out making lists, taking inventory,
organizing the next day, and the day after that.

Is it enough that I give you a body each night?

That I move in close, my knees pressing into
the back of your knees? That I sleep with my arm
around you? Or will I wake one day to find
I've been living in the wrong story? When I close
the book, will I wish I was here with you now?

begonia

Pink-petaled,
tender
folded hearts

on my windowsill,
only for a season.

Is that enough?

One sweet summer,
the exhalation.

Do I lie to myself?

When I say I can
find you again,
know you by the

first petal opening,
by the way
the light strikes you.

Doesn't everyone
need a dream?
Something sweet

to return to,
or wake from,
a reason to go on.

opaque

Either I am loved or I'm not. What use
is it to ask for proof, for signs, for a hand
extended, pointing in the direction of
home? I've imagined everything
or everything is real. Over-simplistic.
But what price would I pay for clarity?
If certainty is held in a palm,
what must I give up in order to hold it?

Yet when I close my eyes I am
walking through the desert, well attended
toward a—*what*? I cannot see it
for the horizon rises above me and the sky
fills with birds. Like my heart, fluttering
sands shift beneath my feet…

Just more dreams? Small comforts
that I give to myself on frosty mornings
when I am most alone, in bed.
When the blue jay in the garden
hasn't yet opened her throat to song. When
all I have is a pounding in my chest
and the knowledge it will stop.

Do I need to know where this rhythm
comes from? Must *I* know who
composed this beat? And for what purpose?
Or can it be enough that I hear music?
That when we are together, we dance?

first snow

It comes down like a dream,
soft edges, slow.

I think of scientists, of
natural order and the instruction
not to confuse results

with causation.
There is *what happens* and
there is *what is possible*.

Do white flakes fall
because they can, they want to?

Or do they manifest
like a wish to fulfill a desire?

What is desire, if not ice
melting on the tongue?

Is life (or love) anything more
than an opportunity seized?

How can I get what I want?

A child and a scientist
will give you different answers.

My real questions:

Did you call me here?
Did you dream up my face,
my lips, these eyes, the way

my hand would feel slipping
into yours? Or did I

come of my own volition?
Am I the dreamer or the dream?

you love me better

When I was asked to imagine
what your soul looked like, what shape
it would take, I saw a white cockatoo,
yellow-crested, with kind, curious eyes.

And let's not forget that you were
the one who first saw the white peacock,
by the road, its plumage long behind it.

Both are steadfast mates full of beautiful
song. And what am I?

Cyanocitta cristata. Bold maybe.
And I can make you laugh.
But is that what you want? Someone

always cutting across the sky? Bright blue
and darting, demanding, someone
with places to go and things to do.

Not to mention a bit of a thief—
shameless
because I'm not the least bit sorry

that I stole your attention, knowing
full well I don't deserve it.
But I do love a challenge, a chance

to prove myself. So let's fly
into the dark. Despite the nighttime
and the creatures that must eat.

Despite the silence descending
like a winter's blanket,
the lone timer ticking off stage.

Let the first flakes fall.
I want to see what winter will
make of you and me.

an egg

misshapen, uneven,
but when you roll it

between your hands
it's potential. Never

mind the crushing
weight of so much

duality. Birth, fruition,
or abrupt endings.

All vie for a place
in this story.

All stories end in death,
they say.

Possibly.
Or they begin with it.

III.

the inevitable

There's a branch from a maple tree.

It hangs low over the sidewalk and
I spring up to greet it, touching its

bark as I pass. I do this for years.
I can leap now without thinking.

One night I go up,
and I find only air, waiting.

Something breathes in the nothing
because grief occupies space, too.

I wonder what it will be like
when I lose you.

while you work in the garden

Love poems often contain flowers
and here I am trying to decide if you are
the first crocus of spring, my first color
after so much white winter.

Or perhaps a daisy, a dahlia—
you too have a radiant face worth
gazing upon.

Could you be hyacinth, or honeysuckle?
Fragrant. As it seems your scent
lingers long after you have left a room.

Or maybe it's only that I cannot stop
thinking of you. Then I see you
unexpectedly rise up in the garden,
dirt on your cheek. I know then
you are a wild bloom, unnameable.

Resplendent in sunlight, I will see
you smiling, just as you are now,
long after I close my eyes.

the end of summer

The leaves are drying up.
The trees, thirsty, know they must soon sleep.

Good night, good night. Sweet dreams, I sing to them.
Share your dreams with me.

We all need rest.

You and I can be no different. But I want to know:
Will you be there when my last leaf curls?

Is it your voice
that will carry me away on the wind?

in the name of love

Tonight we drive a friend to Indiana
in the name of love. How could we not?

What bad karma will we invite
if we refuse to aid her heart
in its longing? I know it seems silly. But

how can we sit safe in our warm house,
while someone begs at the door.

Didn't you know? They wander the night,
so many. They go from door to door to door.
They knock. They ask for fire. For bread.

They are tired of walking. They are tired
of having only their own voices for company.

Meanwhile our clothes are washed. Our bellies
are full. Each night I lay down beside you
and every morning I wake up to your kiss.

Sure, this fire is of our own making. After
all these years, no one is stoking the flame but us.

But aren't we lucky to have the wood?
The kindling? The sturdy hearth in which to build

something more.
More importantly, my love, is the knowing
it will not always be so.

One morning you—or I—will wake.
The fire will be extinguished.
The bed will be cold, emptied. And when—
not if—this happens, only one thing can be done.

The survivor must leave the crumbling house
for the winter night. She must walk the path
alone. From house to house to house, knocking…

But for now we are both alive.
So let's get the keys. Let's be the patron saints
of love. And see where this new road will take us.

first light

Blink and you'll miss us. Each season
has a stillness. In summer, when the wind
lifts the branches, and whispers
old names. In the winter, when all the sound
has been packed beneath the snow
for safe keeping. In the spring, the moment
a magnolia blossom opens, seeking sunbeams.
Fall as the first golden star releases its hold
on its bough and tumbles with nothing
but the faith left in its heart. These moments
are easy to miss. Once gone
they feel like dreams half-remembered.
Aren't we also a moment? The sound
of your key in the door. The way you call out
my name. Lips pulling into a smile just before
we kiss. Even the sweetest dreams will be
forgotten. And when I wake in my next life,
in my next body, will you be there? Or will I
have only the birds to tell me incomprehensible
stories of how once I was loved so well?

thinking ahead

I often imagine those future
versions of ourselves. Don't you?

How will I know you?
By the laugh I love so well?

By the smile I cherish more?
Or are those only special editions?

A limited time offer for my greedy
heart, a treasure box

where I store pleasures
from each life? I can't remember

where I've hidden it and that's
a problem for another day.

How did I fall in love with you
before? Was it a slow dawn

on a fall morning? The cold
frost rising from warm lips?

Was it in a city at night?
With starlight caught in your eyes,

on your cheeks as you turned
toward me smiling? Or maybe

in the way you said my name?
Not the given one—which changes—

but the one I've owned since
all this began. I think you

and the birds are the few
who remember it. I also worry

about whole lives spent
in passing. A glimpse here.

Two words exchanged—and then
perhaps only in a dream.

Were you the girl selling flowers?
Or the boy shining shoes? Or

the one bending the horse's head
so you could whisper gently against

its acquired fears? Don't think
of that now. For now we are together

and you have a lovely face. I hope

mine's not too bad either. See?

When together, it's easy to believe
we always will be. So tell me,

how should we do it? Again, should
I kiss you first? Or maybe

enemies-to-lovers, your favorite trope.
Come here and dream with me.

Let's write the next chapter together
while we still have time.

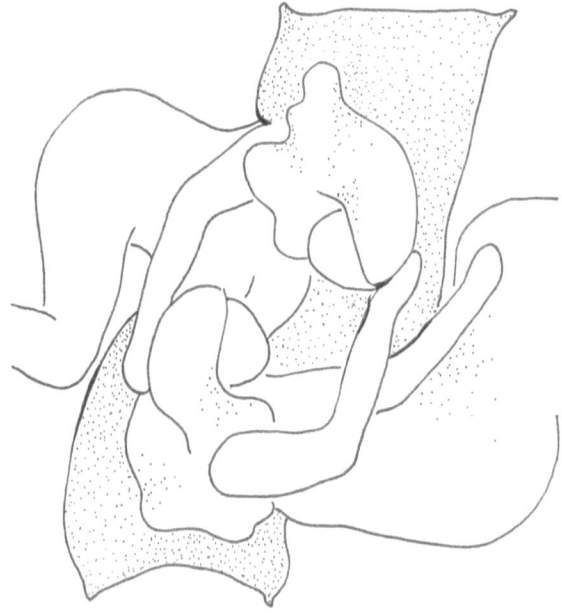

iloilo city

Horns, sirens, music at all hours
of the night. An endless cacophony
of lives in motion. A new world
is created around us. Decay continues
at its side. This says nothing
of the roosters, of the lizards falling
onto your head, of dogs barking,
or the absence of stop signs.

In the chaos, a rhythm.
Sunset is blush pink, orange,
everywhere. On your side
of the world and mine.

When we were children,
didn't the same stars shine and die
above our heads? The same sun rose
each morning. At dawn, dreams
thin like mist in every mind.

What difference does an ocean make?
A fold in dimensional space and time?
What is 8,419 miles to birds,
as long as they know
where they must be by winter?

Why should I be afraid of an imagined

distance, made longer by nightmares
and a skittish mind? I've crossed
great distances before. At least this time,
there are lights. Everywhere.
And they shine even when its dark.

the waking

Tonight, after we had a nice dinner,
I left you safe on the couch.
I took the dog out into the cool
evening. The night was alive
with the smell of linden blossoms
and I was transported
to another night, also in June,
some eleven years before,
in Prague. I had a small apartment.
I often walked. There was also linden.
But I was lonely and alone then.
I had not yet finished writing a novel,
which is to say, I still had all
my sadness inside of me.
I ate gnocchi. I cried
at a wobbly desk in a barren room.
I wrote poems Murakami
would be proud of,
had I not burned them. Dramatically,
I don't remember much except for
the sadness. For the way it hung
in the air like accordion music, how
it smelled like rain on car tires.
How I was so empty it hurt.
Longing is a nightmare, not a hunger
and once you wake with someone's
arms around you, you can't be sure
if you slept at all.

first date

It wasn't a discovery so much
as a remembering. When you
stepped onto the curb, my heart
said something like, "Oh yes,
here she is." As if you'd slipped
from the room
while I was preoccupied, only
to return the moment I began
to *really* miss you. The romance,
too, that followed was like a Satie
melody I danced to long ago.
It didn't matter that the era
had changed, the fashion. I knew
who my dance partner was. And
these thoughts give me great comfort,
that when the missing you is over,
it will be like I'd never missed you at all.
An infinity of loneliness will blink out
of existence. I understand that this
is also true: one night you'll release
my hand. The music will end and I'll
be left, waiting, for it to begin again.

grief

It hurt more than walking barefoot
through a field of frost, onto a trail
so narrow as if for only one soul.
Birch sentinels in white uniforms
marred by black patches stood guard.
I thought they would not let me pass,
so I told them about the girl
who grew sunflowers. I told them
they could have the plates.
They could have the queen-sized bed,
far too big for the one body left behind.
*And you can have the last of what I
remember—of this love, this life.*

For this, they moved aside.

Once there were brilliant orange
and red starbursts. Now what was left
was brown, shriveled, tossed about.

I went deep into the forest like a fugitive,
like a refugee, but there is no refuge
when what is broken is carried within you.
And the legs do not give up as soon
as you'd like them to.

I wanted to go out there and die, like

an old dog who knew her time had come.

It was the moon who changed my mind.
She knows something of long nights.
She has a way of meeting your eye,
of speaking with a nightjar's trill, stating
gently: *Like it or not, dawn always comes.*

the leap

We gather at the cliffs.
We manage the ascent
though we know what's coming.
Pine branches are fragrant
in the night. Our bright
chattering like birds is meant
to hide everything from fear
to inadequacy. It doesn't matter
if we've done this before.
It doesn't matter if we plan
to jump this time with our hands
twined with another's.
The truth is absolute:

It is a hard climb
and you are expected
to jump willingly at the end of it.

All of your friends are doing it.
You don't want to be the last one—
or the first. Of course it happens
in the dark. You aren't supposed to
see where this is going.
You must have faith
there is water below and that
nothing in the water is hungry.

Open your arms now.

Leave what you don't need behind.
When you break the surface again, *if*
you breathe again,
the fear will be behind you.
You'll hear only relieved laughter,
a sweet voice calling you to shore.

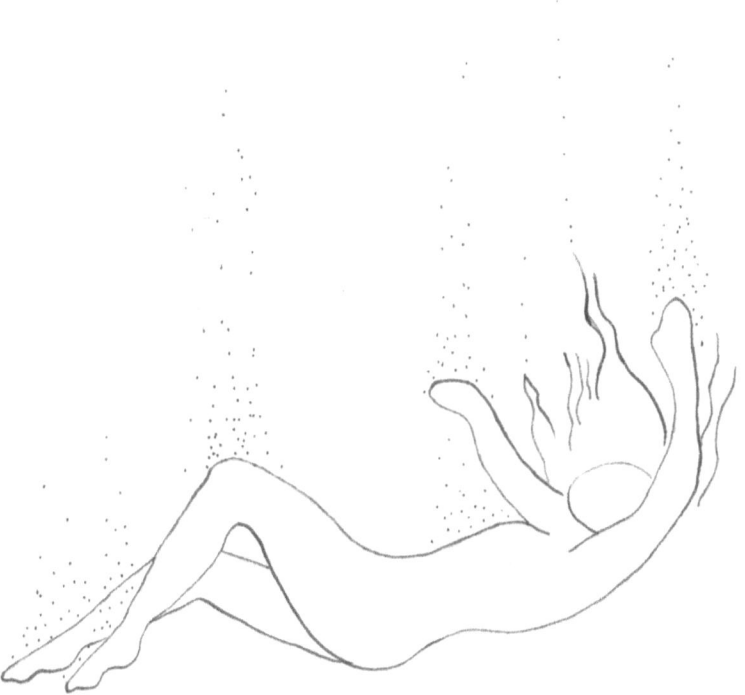

white crane

She snaps open her wings, falls
from a high branch. She glides, coasting
above the thrashing river.

It's always one step, isn't it? Only one step.
One moment. Between this life and the next.

the wind

One whisper
and the branches lift.
One request
and the water ripples
dancing to the rhythm
of my song.
Now, whenever I like I can
push back the hair
from your face. Without
a body, I can move
seen and unseen.

It takes losing one's self,
one's form,
to understand all those
feelings of *not enough*
never enough
more
more

Only when one is limitless
again
does one understand
small. As a pebble it is

easy to forget you
were once a mountain.

The wind knows
nothing of separation.

It will teach us
how to begin again.

how I knew

The morning the squirrel shat on me,
you were the one I called
first. Not because you could help,
living as you were,
eighty miles away, but
because I knew I could surprise
a laugh out of you.
Or maybe it was before that, when
dreaming, I had asked,
"Is there anyone waiting for me?"
And the dream girl replied, "I am."
That was good enough. In truth,
this life is like that movie,
where the girl forgets her man every
night. And he must convince her
that she loves him. Again. Each day.
Which is to say, every life I discover
you, a conch shell with a new coil.
And when pressed to my ear, I hear
the first notes of a beloved song.

evening star

You don't walk with me
in the evenings, in purple twilight. It suits us.

It's a truthful portrayal. We both know
I am the restless one.

I must go farther on my own two feet
before I am granted permission to rest.

When I wander, I think of you sometimes.
Or I turn words, like those in this poem,

over like a puzzle box in my mind.
We all have our jobs

and the way we like to do them.
When I see couples walking, hand-in-hand,

I smile, catch the falling pieces
of their conversations like torn-up violets

on the pavement. That's one way to do it.
Together, heads bent.

But I don't mind our fashion. I like it,
when tired, I round the corner and find

the light is on. And you in the lit window,
wanting, and ready to open the door.

love through the ages

It's true that there is so much to distract.
Even when I am completely alone
in a silent office, at home, there are bills,
a dog snoring, a chime at the door.

A memory can surface suddenly and I'll try
to remember who was with me that night,
while the birds sustained a melody.

All of this pulls at the legs.
The heart and the mind are currents.

In such an existence, if we aren't careful,
it would be easy to drift away
from one another. Yet tonight,
under the full moon, I see two trees.

Tall, proud, and in their manner, quite
separate, with a river of concrete poured
between them.

But even with the new houses popping up,
the newer cars passing by, the families living
and dying around them, they seek each other.

However fixed in their own soils, they still
defy the night. Not only under the concrete,

with roots gently twining, but also

in the light. Each leaf stretching across
the sky is a hand reaching,
their branches brimming with bird song—

And that's enough.

This is the thought I will hold onto
as I make my way home to you.

author's note

Dear reader,

I hope you enjoyed my foray into love poetry. If you would be so kind, please leave a review for this collection on whichever retail sites you prefer.

It would mean so much to me, and to the other poetry lovers who may discover this collection because of your review. Not to mention reviews are one of the best ways to support the writers and artists you love.

If you want more poems, you can visit me at
https://www.korymshrum.com/free-starter-library

For more art from the amazing, Victoria Solomon, you can follow her on Instagram @victoriamsolomon

On my website, you can also sign up for my newsletter and receive a free poetry chapbook. The newsletter will be sent 2-3 times a month and contain free poems and updates about my work. I will never share your email and, of course, you can unsubscribe at any time.

Hope to chat with you soon!

k.b. marie

also by k.b. marie

birds & other dreamers

questions for the dead

you can't keep it

about the author

K.B. Marie has published over thirty poems in magazines such as *Bateau, North American Review, Ascent,* and elsewhere under the name, Kory M. Shrum. She earned her MFA at Western Michigan University and has worked for *New Issues Press, Zone 3 Press,* and *Third Coast Literary Magazine.*

For ten years, she taught writing to thousands of university students before deciding to write full-time. Her favorite kind of poetry combines art and words – which is why her work is often accompanied with illustrations or other visuals.

She lives in Michigan with her equally well-read wife, Kimberly, and their rescue pug, Charley.

Anything else you'd like to know can be found at https://www.korymshrum.com/poetry

about the illustrator

Victoria Solomon is a Michigan-based artist specializing in pencil and ink portraiture and other art. When not powering through nursing school, she loves to experiment with new art supplies and write fiction. She also makes an incredible chocolate cake. Victoria shares her home with her husband and her small brood of children and cats.

Follow her on Instagram @victoriamsolomon

www.ingramcontent.com/pod-product-compliance
Lightning Source LLC
Chambersburg PA
CBHW030157100526
44592CB00009B/323